Spies
and
Codebreakers

CLAIRE THROP

Raintree is an imprint of Capstone Global Library Limited, a company incorporated in England and Wales having its registered office at 7 Pilgrim Street, London, EC4V 6LB – Registered company number: 6695582

www.raintree.co.uk
myorders@raintree.co.uk

Text © Capstone Global Library Limited 2016
The moral rights of the proprietor have been asserted.

Edited by Helen Cox Cannons
Designed by Philippa Jenkins
Original illustrations © Capstone Global Library Limited 2015
Illustrated by HL Studios, Witney, Oxon
Picture research by Jo Miller
Production by Helen McCreath
Originated by Capstone Global Library Limited
Printed and bound in China

ISBN 978 1 406 29882 6 (hardback)
19 18 17 16 15
10 9 8 7 6 5 4 3 2 1

ISBN 978 1 406 29887 1 (paperback)
20 19 18 17 16
10 9 8 7 6 5 4 3 2 1

British Library Cataloguing in Publication Data
A full catalogue record for this book is available from the British Library.

Acknowledgements
We would like to thank the following for permission to reproduce photographs: Alamy: Chris Dorney, 41, famouspeople, cover (right), INTERFOTO, 23, INTERFOTO, cover (left), Stuart Robertson, 24, Tim E White, 29; CIA, 20; Corbis, 37, Hulton-Deutsch Collection, 19; Dreamstime: Mike_kiev, 1; Getty Images: AFP/STF, 17, Evening Standard, 25, Fotosearch, 39, Keystone, 13, Popperfoto, 11, 27, Popperfoto/Paul Popper, 7, Roger Viollet, 36, Roger Viollet/Lipnitzki, 10, SSPL, 31, The LIFE Picture Collection/National Archives, 28; Library of Congress: Elias Goldensky, 12, Mennonite Archives of Ontario/David Hunsberger, 33; Newscom: akg-images, 8, 9, NI Syndication, 6, SIPA/Universal Photo, 22, ZUMA Press/Coby Burns, 26, ZUMA Press/Keystone Pictures USA, 18, ZUMA Press/Solo, 35; Shutterstock: Alexey Arkhipov, 16; SuperStock: Science and Society, cover (background), The Image Works: Sueddeutsche Zeitung Photo/S.M., 30; The National Archives of the UK, 14; Wikimedia: Alison Wheeler, 34, Matt Crypto, 32, U.S. Navy, 38.

The heroes featured on the front cover are Barbara Lauwers (left) and Alan Turing (right).

We would like to thank Nick Hunter for his invaluable help in the preparation of this book.

Every effort has been made to contact copyright holders of material reproduced in this book. Any omissions will be rectified in subsequent printings if notice is given to the publisher.

Contents

The story of World War II

Germany, under the leadership of Adolf Hitler, invaded Poland on
1 September 1939. Two days later, Britain and France declared war on
Germany. This is how World War II began. What many thought would
last six weeks continued for six long years. Without the efforts of brave
codebreakers and spies, the war might have lasted even longer.

BLITZKRIEG

During May and June 1940, the Nazis overpowered Belgium, the
Netherlands and France in just six weeks, in what became known as
Blitzkrieg (lightning war). Thousands of British troops were evacuated to
safety from Dunkirk, France. On 10 June 1940, Italy entered the war on
the side of the Axis Powers. Four days later, the Nazis took France's capital
city, Paris. Britain was now the only one of the Allies left to fight Germany.

AXIS POWERS VERSUS THE ALLIES

The Axis Powers included Germany (the Nazis), Italy (for part
of the war), and later Japan. These countries fought against the
Allies. The Allies included Britain, France, the Soviet Union
(from June 1941) and, from December 1941, the United States.

This map shows how much of Europe and the USSR was occupied by the Axis Powers by 1941. The map also shows the cities that were badly damaged by bombing raids.

0   250   500 miles

0   250   500 kilometres

N
W   E
S

ATLANTIC OCEAN

Finland
Norway   Sweden
Leningrad
Estonia
North Sea   Denmark   Latvia
Great Britain   Lithuania   Moscow
Netherlands   East Prussia
Liverpool   Hull   Berlin   Warsaw
Ireland   Manchester   USSR (SOVIET UNION)
Bristol   London   Rotterdam
Plymouth   Belg.   Germany   Poland   Extent of Axis advance, 1941
Southampton   Dunkirk   Lux.   Czechoslovakia   Stalingrad
Paris   Munich
France   Switz.   Austria   Hungary
Extent of Axis advance, 1940   Romania
Vichy France   Belgrade   Black Sea
Italy   Yugoslavia
Portugal   Spain   Rome   Bulgaria
Albania
Mediterranean Sea   Greece   Turkey
Malta
Morocco   Tunisia
Algeria
Libya

Axis, 1939
Axis-controlled, 1941
Allies
Neutral
Axis advances
Cities severely damaged by bombing

THE BLITZ

The bombing of Britain – known as the Blitz – began in September 1940. After the Nazis failed to beat the Royal Air Force in the Battle of Britain, Hitler ordered the dropping of bombs on major British cities and industrial areas. If the Nazis had hoped to destroy the spirits of the British people, they failed. Instead, the British pulled together while sheltering from the bombs.

MORE COUNTRIES JOIN THE WAR

In June 1941, Germany invaded the Soviet Union in what was known as Operation Barbarossa. This brought the huge Soviet army into the war. On 7 December, Japanese aeroplanes attacked the US naval base at Pearl Harbor, Hawaii, a disaster that wasn't anticipated. The United States entered the war one day later.

In World War II, women took on jobs previously held by men. Here, members of the Women's Auxiliary Air Force are working on a lorry.

THE TEHRAN CONFERENCE

The Tehran Conference took place in Iran from 28 November to 1 December 1943. It was the first time that the leaders of Britain, the Soviet Union and the United States had come together. They discussed three main topics:

1. British prime minister Winston Churchill and US president Franklin D. Roosevelt agreed to invade France the following year, beginning with the D-Day landings on Normandy's beaches.

2. The Soviets, led by Joseph Stalin, would step up the fighting on the Eastern Front, which would split the Nazi forces across two fronts. They also agreed to join the war against Japan after Germany was defeated.

3. The three leaders decided to set up a new international organization to try to keep peace around the world. This organization became the United Nations.

Three world leaders – Stalin, Roosevelt and Churchill (left to right) – worked together to fight the Nazis.

This aerial view shows the destruction in Berlin, Germany, at the end of the war.

CODEBREAKING

Meanwhile, hundreds of codebreakers were working to decipher Nazi messages sent over the airwaves. In early 1942, the Nazis created a new, more complicated code. The world's first semi-programmable computer – called Colossus – was in action at Bletchley Park, England, by December 1943. This sped up the codebreaking process.

D-DAY

D-Day was the start of a major attack on Nazi-occupied Europe. On 6 June 1944, the Allies crossed the English Channel to land on the beaches of Normandy, France. The Allies had kept the location of the attack secret by using double agents, such as Garbo (see pages 14–17), to persuade the Nazis that the planned landing site was Pas de Calais. In fact, it was further south in Normandy. This meant that far fewer Nazis were in Normandy to face the Allied troops. The Allies slowly progressed until the Germans in Paris surrendered on 25 August 1944.

THE END OF THE WAR

In April 1945, the Soviet army marched into Berlin, where Hitler was based. Hitler took his own life rather than be captured by the Soviets. Berlin had suffered two years of bombing by British and US planes, and now faced total destruction by the Soviets.

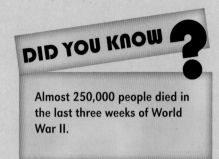
The war in Europe finally ended on 8 May 1945. VE (Victory in Europe) Day parties took place all over Europe.

The war against Japan continued, however. It was the dropping of atomic bombs on the Japanese cities Hiroshima and Nagasaki in August that eventually forced Japan to surrender. VJ (Victory over Japan) Day was celebrated on 15 August 1945.

People in New York, USA, celebrated the end of the war on VJ Day, 15 August 1945.

The need for secrecy

During wartime, it is vital that messages containing information about invasion and battle plans are kept secret. Undercover agents, or spies, were used by most countries in the war. Some became double agents. This is when an agent agreed to spy for one side while actually reporting back to the other side. They sometimes gave the enemy false information. This dangerous work helped the Allies to fool the Nazis about their plans for D-Day.

SECURITY SERVICE

The Security Service, also known as MI5, focused on protecting Britain against foreign spies. MI5 was able to capture most German spies who entered Britain during the war and turned many of them into double agents. This was known as the Double Cross system.

It is thought that French fashion designer Coco Chanel was an Abwehr spy.

In 1942, an MI5 plot to uncover British supporters of the Nazis revealed hundreds of sympathizers. An MI5 agent, known only as Jack King, contacted a woman called Marita Perigoe, who had a network of Nazi supporters. King told her he was a member of the Gestapo, the German Secret Police, and that he needed agents who would be willing to help Germany when it invaded Britain. Perigoe was willing to help and saw King as her link to the Nazis. By the end of the war, MI5 was secretly in control of a large number of Nazi supporters who believed that they were working for the Nazis.

THE ABWEHR

The Abwehr was a German intelligence-gathering organization in operation until 1944. In July of that year, the Abwehr was shut down. This was after a plot to kill Hitler, involving the Abwehr's leader, Wilhelm Canaris (above), had failed.

Franklin D. Roosevelt was the US president from 1933 until 1945.

SECRET INTELLIGENCE SERVICE

The British Secret Intelligence Service (SIS) – also known as MI6 – dealt with British spies in foreign countries. Existing SIS networks in Europe were badly damaged during the early part of the war as the Nazis occupied more and more countries, but they soon began to be repaired as opposition to Hitler and the Nazis increased.

SIS also oversaw the work of the Government Code and Cipher School (see page 25). Coded messages were deciphered and the information passed to SIS. It then sent the information to Allied commanders.

OFFICE OF STRATEGIC SERVICES

The Office of Strategic Services (OSS) was set up in June 1942 by US president Franklin D. Roosevelt to find information on the enemy (Germany and Japan), and to sabotage their military plans. At its peak, OSS had 24,000 employees. OSS had close links with the British intelligence services.

LOOSE AND CARELESS TALK

A fear of spies running around Britain and reporting what they overheard to the Nazis led to a "Careless Talk" poster campaign. This was to warn people of the problems that might occur if sensitive information got into Nazi hands. Posters included ones showing people chatting, with images of Hitler hidden in the wallpaper or in paintings on the wall (see below). Later, a "Loose Talk" campaign took place in the United States. Posters included one that read "Loose lips might sink ships".

There were many brave volunteers who worked as Allied spies during the war. The following pages tell the stories of just a few.

Don't forget that walls have ears!

Garbo

G̲arbo's real name was Juan Pujol. He was born in Barcelona, Spain, in 1912. Some have said that he was the most successful double agent of the war. He fought in the Spanish Civil War (1936–39) and as a result of this experience had a strong dislike of dictators (people who have total control over a country), such as Hitler

OFFERING TO BE A BRITISH SPY

In January 1941, Pujol tried - unsuccessfully - to make contact with the British to offer his services as a spy. Eventually, he decided that the British might accept him if he was already spying for the Nazis and had gained their trust. Pujol managed to persuade an agent from the Abwehr, the German intelligence service, that he had a visa that allowed him to travel to Britain. He offered to go there and spy for the Nazis. They accepted and trained him to become an Abwehr agent.

But Pujol's visa was not real, so he wasn't actually able to travel to Britain. He based himself in Lisbon, Portugal. From October 1941, he began supplying reports to the Nazis based on information from his network of agents in Britain. However, none of the agents was real! He made up stories of trips around Britain and of the narrow escapes he and his agents had. While Pujol made some errors about Britain, the Nazis came to fully trust his misleading reports.

DID YOU KNOW?

Pujol had never even visited Britain at the time he was supposedly there spying for the Nazis! He used books and magazines at Lisbon Public Library to make his reports sound real.

SPYING FOR THE BRITISH

Pujol finally managed to make contact with the British in early 1942. He was invited to London and given a handler to work with, the Spanish-speaking Tomás Harris. He and Harris wrote 315 letters that contained a secret form of writing. These letters supposedly came from Pujol's network of 27 completely made-up spies. As a result, the Nazis did not bother to send any other spies to Britain.

OPERATION FORTITUDE

Pujol had an important role in the success of Operation Fortitude. Operation Fortitude was a trick played on the Nazis about where the D-Day landings would take place. In January 1944, the Nazis told Pujol that they thought the Allies were preparing to invade. He was asked to find out more.

DID YOU KNOW ?

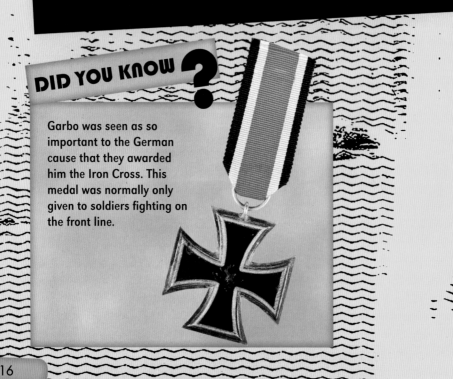

Garbo was seen as so important to the German cause that they awarded him the Iron Cross. This medal was normally only given to soldiers fighting on the front line.

These US soldiers are arriving on the beaches of Normandy on D-Day, 6 June 1944.

The Allies did have a plan to invade Europe but this included fooling the Nazis about where exactly they would land. Pujol told the Nazis that the Allies were going to invade Europe from Calais. This was where Hitler thought they would land. In fact, they landed on the beaches of Normandy. Pujol even told the Nazis that the Normandy landings were just a trick to put them off the main attack at Calais. The Nazis accepted this information as trustworthy. They even kept troops at Calais during July and August in preparation for the attack that never came.

Agent Zigzag

Agent Zigzag (real name Eddie Chapman, shown above) was a criminal who made money by blowing up safes in robberies. When the Nazis invaded the Channel Islands in July 1940, Chapman was in prison on the island of Jersey.

Chapman was so desperate to get off the island that he offered to spy for the Nazis. The Abwehr accepted him, thinking that Chapman's skills with explosives would be useful for sabotaging factories, such as the de Havilland aircraft factory. It was there that the British made the Mosquito bomber plane. After training, Chapman was codenamed Fritzchen and sent to England in 1942.

DOUBLE AGENT

MI5 had decoded messages from the Abwehr, so they knew when and where Chapman would be dropped into Britain. After capturing the spy, MI5 told him he had to work for them as a double agent or he would be executed. In January 1943, MI5 and Chapman faked an attack on the de Havilland aircraft factory so that the Nazis would not realize that Chapman had been captured. On his return to Germany, Chapman was awarded the Iron Cross for his sabotage efforts.

A RETURN TO BRITAIN

Chapman was sent back to Britain to report on the German bombing raids. He reported that the Nazis were overshooting their targets, but this wasn't really the case. After the Nazis made alterations, many of their bombs landed in Kent rather than London, causing less damage and fewer deaths.

DID YOU KNOW ?

The fake attack on the aircraft factory was created by covering the buildings in sheets. They painted the sheets to look from the air like the almost destroyed buildings of the factory. The Nazis were fooled by this!

US spies

Born in 1914 in what was then Czechoslovakia, Barbara Lauwers became a lawyer. She married an American and moved to the United States in 1941. On 1 June 1943, she became an American citizen and immediately joined the US Army. After basic training, she was picked to join the OSS.

OPERATION SAUERKRAUT

Lauwers started her OSS career in Algeria, but she was transferred to Rome, Italy, when the Allies entered the city. In summer 1944, Lauwers was chosen to interview prisoners because she could speak many languages: German, English, Czech, Slovak and French. She recruited some of the German prisoners to hand out "black", or negative, propaganda about Hitler behind enemy lines. This was known as Operation Sauerkraut, and its aim was to destroy the German army's spirit. The returning prisoners provided good-quality intelligence and the operation was a success. This system continued throughout the war in Italy and later in France.

In April 1945, 600 Czech soldiers in Italy chose to stop fighting for Hitler and join the Allies. This was a result of the work carried out by Lauwers and her team, who had distributed leaflets that encouraged soldiers forced to fight for the Nazis to leave and join the Allied army. Many of the 600 soldiers were carrying Lauwers' leaflets in their pockets. Lauwers received a Bronze Star medal for her work.

"Only upon arrival [in Washington] were we told that we were assigned to the OSS. Immediately we were [told] to work and keep quiet about it, mind your own business and don't ask questions, be available 24 hours a day, seven days a week."

Barbara Lauwers

CELEBRITY SPIES

In 2008, the OSS revealed that a number of famous people had worked for it during the war. These included the singer and dancer Josephine Baker and chef Julia Childs.

Josephine Baker toured in France and noted, on pieces of paper she then attached to her underwear, anything she overheard that might be important to the Allies! She also wrote secret notes in the lines of her sheet music. She passed on this information to members of the French resistance who came to her shows.

Julia Childs had wanted to join the US Navy but was too tall at 1.8 metres (6 feet 2 inches). Instead, she took a job at the OSS and was based in Washington, DC, during the early part of the war, then later at the OSS office in China.

After the war, Josephine Baker was awarded the Croix de Guerre (Cross of War) medal by the French government for her resistance work.

GERMAN SPIES

Elyesa Bazna (1904–70), who worked for the British ambassador to Turkey, spied for the Nazis from 1943 to 1944. Known as Cicero, he photographed secret documents from the Embassy safe, including information about D-Day. Hitler paid large sums of money for the information, but the Nazis never really trusted Cicero, so they didn't act on his findings.

German-born Waldemar Othmer went to the United States in 1919. He visited Germany in 1937 and was impressed with Hitler's ideas, so offered to spy for the Nazis. In 1940, he got a job at a military base in Virginia, USA, allowing him to pass on information about British and US ships and when they were sailing. Eventually, he was arrested after asking his dentist for a European painkiller that was used to make invisible ink, which he had been using to write to his Nazi handlers.

Codebreakers

Radio communications were essential during war to pass on information, instructions and battle plans. However, radio messages could be secretly listened to, so it was vital that they were disguised using a code. All countries coded their messages and they all hoped their codes wouldn't be broken. Some countries were better at creating stronger codes than others and some were better at breaking codes than others.

Most people at Bletchley Park worked in huts like this one.

CODES AND CIPHERS

- Codes make a message secret by changing whole words into other words or symbols.
- Ciphers make a message secret by rearranging or changing the letters within words into different letters or symbols.

GREAT BRITAIN

Before World War II, there had been two codebreaking units – one for the army and one for the navy – but in 1919, they were brought together to become the Government Code and Cipher School (GC&CS). In 1939, GC&CS moved into Bletchley Park, Buckinghamshire, also known as Station X. The main employees of GC&CS were linguists – people who are good with languages. Later, mathematicians, particularly those also good at chess, were recruited. As the war continued and more people worked at Station X, it became clear that they needed more room. A number of huts were built around the grounds. Each hut was known only by its number. GC&CS increased in size rapidly through the war: by 1942, it had a staff of 1,500 people.

Members of MI6 and GC&CS visited Bletchley Park in August 1938 to see if it would be suitable for wartime intelligence work.

DID YOU KNOW ?

In May 2014, a photograph of the women who worked on Colossus (see pages 34–35) at Bletchley Park resulted in a reunion of some of those women. The photo had been found in a desk drawer. It had not been seen since the war.

Y STATIONS

Y stations, or listening stations, existed around Britain and in other countries. People listened to enemy messages 24 hours a day. They would then pass the messages to Bletchley Park to decipher. Around 4,000 coded messages came into Bletchley Park every day. The information gathered from the decoded messages was known as Ultra – it was top secret. Each person usually saw only part of a message before passing it on to someone else.

Radios like these were used at Y stations across the country. Listeners picked up messages sent in Morse Code (code in long and short sounds), wrote them down and sent them to Bletchley Park.

This aircraft carrier, HMS *Ark Royal*, was part of the British navy during World War II.

SIGNALS INTELLIGENCE SERVICE, USA

In the United States, the Signals Intelligence Service was part of the army. It mainly prepared codes for the army to use and trained codebreakers for when the United States entered the war. OP-20-G was the cryptography unit of the navy. This unit focused on decoding messages sent by the Japanese navy. The information that came through these two units was called Magic. The Navajo code-talkers were another important part of the United States intelligence service (see page 37).

GERMAN CODEBREAKING SUCCESS

The Nazis had some success at codebreaking themselves. They decoded the British naval code in 1935, which gave them success in the early part of the Battle of the Atlantic, which lasted throughout the war. In 1941, decoding secret messages sent by the British navy allowed the Nazis to destroy 875 Allied ships. Later, the Nazis were able to crack the codes of the Soviets and Danes.

The Enigma machine

The Enigma machine was invented by the Germans in 1918. The German navy first used it to send coded messages in 1926, but later the army and air force also used it.

These Nazi soldiers are using the Enigma machine to send coded messages.

Enigma worked by changing the letters of an ordinary message (called plaintext) into an encrypted, or coded, message. It had a keyboard of 26 letters and a lampboard with small windows showing letters that would light up, one at a time, as the keys on the keyboard were pressed. Wheels attached to a scrambler unit would move around so that the letter that lit up on the lampboard was not the same letter that had been pressed on the keyboard. This was how Enigma produced a coded message.

POLISH HELP

While the British had thought that Enigma was unbreakable, Polish codebreakers had been deciphering German messages for years. Mathematicians Marian Rejewski, Henryk Zygalski and Jerzy Rozycki made the first breakthrough in deciphering the Enigma code in 1938, with the help of photos of an operating manual taken by the French Secret Service and a German traitor. However, at that time the cipher changed once every few months. Once the war started, it changed at least once a day. In the end, there were not enough Polish codebreakers to complete the work.

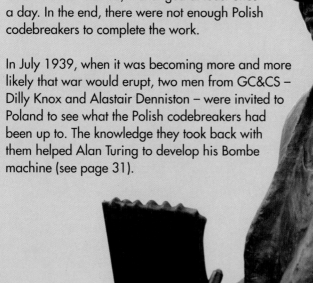

This statue of Marian Rejewski is in Poland. A Polish Day is now held every year at Bletchley Park to celebrate the Polish codebreakers, whose work was previously unrecognized.

In July 1939, when it was becoming more and more likely that war would erupt, two men from GC&CS – Dilly Knox and Alastair Denniston – were invited to Poland to see what the Polish codebreakers had been up to. The knowledge they took back with them helped Alan Turing to develop his Bombe machine (see page 31).

Alan Turing

Alan Turing was born in London in 1912. He went to Cambridge University to study – and later teach – maths. It was here that he came up with the proof that is now thought to be the basis of all computers.

In 1936, Turing went to Princeton University in the United States, where he began to study ciphers. He returned to Britain two years later. It was around this time that he began to secretly work for GC&CS. When the war began, he moved to the GC&CS headquarters at Bletchley Park.

BOMBE MACHINE

Turing led a team that developed a Bombe machine that by May 1940 could decrypt German Air Force messages sent through Enigma. Polish codebreakers had come up with the idea of the Bombe but Turing improved it. His version used known or guessed parts of the message – known as cribs – to help decipher it. The Bombe tried all the possible Enigma wheel positions so that there were fewer settings that needed to be tested by people. German navy messages were far more difficult to break. Turing had broken the code system at the end of 1939, but regular decryption wasn't possible until mid-1941, after the British navy captured Enigma machines and code books.

AFTER THE WAR

Working at the National Physical Laboratory after the war, Turing began to develop a machine that could process information, known as the Automatic Computing Engine (ACE). Unfortunately, the other people he worked with did not support his ideas, and he lost the chance to create a digital computer at his laboratory. Turing continued to work in the field of computing until his death in 1954.

This is the Bombe machine used to decipher early Enigma codes.

The Tunny machine

This Lorenz machine can be seen at Bletchley Park Museum.

In 1941, Y listeners began to notice a new sound – it turned out to be messages delivered by teleprinter rather than Morse code. The Lorenz SZ40/42 was used by the German army. It was a more complex machine than Enigma, which had become slow and outdated even by the start of World War II. The Lorenz, known as Tunny by those working at Bletchley Park, encoded messages twice by using five wheels and then five more. Two extra wheels added randomness to the code, which meant they couldn't be predicted. This resulted in 1.6 million billion possible combinations.

The breakthrough came when a German Lorenz operator made a mistake. On 30 August 1941, he sent a particularly long message from Athens to Vienna, but the receiver didn't get the whole message and asked for it to be sent again. The operator failed to change the wheel setting. He also abbreviated words so the message wasn't exactly the same. This gave the Bletchley Park codebreakers a bigger sample to work with.

JOHN TILTMAN AND WILLIAM TUTTE

Over 10 days, John Tiltman, one of the best codebreakers at Bletchley Park, deciphered the German operator's message. William Tutte (shown below) then worked out the main structure of the machine from the message deciphered by Tiltman. Other researchers joined in and they soon knew the way the Tunny machine worked, which was an impressive achievement, considering nobody in Britain had ever seen one.

HEATH ROBINSON

Working out the wheel patterns on Tunny would allow the Allies to read the German messages. Again, in November 1942, William Tutte came up with the answer. Heath Robinson was the nickname of the machine that was produced to put Tutte's ideas into action. While it did speed up the process, the machine kept breaking down.

COLOSSUS

Tommy Flowers, a General Post Office engineer, was asked to repair Heath Robinson. However, he said he could build a machine that could decipher messages faster than Heath Robinson, using electronic circuits and valves. This machine was Colossus, the world's first semi-programmable computer.

This is Heath Robinson, William Tutte's codebreaking machine.

In 2007, a working copy of Colossus went on display at the National Museum of Computing at Bletchley Park.

Flowers and his team built the first Colossus, Mark 1, in just 11 months. It was demonstrated – and worked! – in December 1943, and was transferred to Bletchley Park the following month. Colossus could read 5,000 characters a minute compared to Heath Robinson's 1,000. Work had already started on Colossus Mark 2, so it was ready by June – just in time for D-Day. It helped the Allies to discover that the Nazis had fallen for Operation Fortitude (see page 16). Amazingly, the Nazis did not know that their code had been broken and that the Allies were listening in to top-secret conversations.

DID YOU KNOW ?

Because of the secrecy surrounding the work at Bletchley Park, it was many years before anyone heard about Colossus. In 1948, the Americans announced that they had created the first digital computer – ENIAC. Only a few people knew that this was not the case – Tommy Flowers had created the first one five years before.

US codebreaking

In February 1939, US codebreakers discovered that the Japanese had started using a new cipher machine. It became known as Purple. A team, led by Frank Rowlett, worked on deciphering the machine's messages. In September 1940, cryptanalyst Genevieve Grotjan Feinstein made the breakthrough. This helped the Signals Intelligence Service build a machine called Purple Analog that could quickly decipher the Japanese messages from Purple. Intelligence from Purple was extremely helpful for the Allies because it contained information that the Japanese requested from the other Axis Powers.

Japanese soldiers attacked on the Eastern Front.

ELIZEBETH AND WILLIAM FRIEDMAN

Elizebeth and William Friedman were US codebreakers. William was the better known – he ran the Signals Intelligence Service – and helped to break a Japanese cipher, but it was Elizebeth who introduced him to codebreaking. She was involved in decoding messages from the Doll Woman, a Japanese spy whose real name was Velvalee Dickinson, owner of a doll shop in New York City, USA.

William Friedman demonstrates a cipher machine to another member of his team.

THE NAVAJO CODE-TALKERS

In 1942, the US military recruited 29 Native Americans from the Navajo tribe to create a code that they could use to secretly transmit battle plans. The Navajo language was thought to be too difficult for anyone other than a person who had grown up with the Navajos to understand. Some words that would be used in coded messages did not exist in Navajo, so they used coded words instead. For example, the word for battleship was "whale". By the end of the war, 420 Navajo men worked as code-talkers. After the war, the Japanese admitted that while they broke other US naval codes, they never managed to decipher the Navajo code.

SIGABA

The first SIGABA machine was built by the US army in 1935. The army shared its design with the navy, although the navy called its machine ECM-MK 1. SIGABA machines produced code used for very high-level communication, such as that between the US president and the British prime minister, Winston Churchill. The system was first used in August 1941. The codes were so secret that even British personnel (those working for the armed forces) were never allowed access to the machine. There were 10,000 SIGABA machines in use by 1943.

This is a SIGABA machine.

SIGABA was much more secure than Enigma. It was similar in that it used wheels, or rotors, to scramble messages. However, whereas Enigma used three or four rotors, SIGABA had 15. It meant there were many more possible combinations of characters. The SIGABA machine was also easier to use, as it only required one person to operate it, whereas Enigma needed someone to type in the original message and another person to record the scrambled message.

Special codebreakers were even asked to attack their own machines in order to test them. SIGABA codes were never broken by the enemy – it was the only cipher machine not to be broken during World War II.

Frank Rowlett (circled), who worked for the Signals Intelligence Service, was one of the creators of SIGABA.

THINK

NO ADMITTANC

This map shows how Europe was divided at the end of World War II, in 1945. Germany was split, as was its capital Berlin.

The work of incredibly intelligent codebreakers, spies and double agents who were brave enough to risk their lives, had a huge impact on the events of World War II. Who knows what the outcome of the war would have been without their remarkable efforts.

DID YOU KNOW ?

By the end of the war, 63 million characters of German communications had been deciphered by 550 people and 10 Colossus computers.

SECRECY ESSENTIAL

The Allies had to be careful about using the intelligence they gathered. They couldn't be too obvious or the Nazis would realize that their codes had been broken. To hide the fact that Enigma had indeed been broken, an MI6 spy network was created. Winston Churchill once wrote to a spy called Boniface to congratulate him on the information he provided, but the spy wasn't actually a real person!

Secrecy was maintained by everyone until the 1970s, and some information about the war is still kept secret. For example, people had to keep the fact they had worked at Bletchley Park from the rest of their family.

SHORTENING THE WAR

Some experts think that the war was shortened by up to two years and that many tens of thousands of lives were saved through the contribution of codebreakers and the use of Colossus. Double agents provided further information, allowing the Allies to control much of the later stages of the war. The Nazis were unaware that spies had access to Hitler's own top-secret messages.

This is a monument to the codebreakers who worked so hard at Bletchley Park during the war.

Timeline

1938
JANUARY FEBRUARY MARCH APRIL MAY JUNE

12 MARCH Germany invades Austria

1939
JANUARY FEBRUARY MARCH APRIL MAY JUNE

15 MARCH Germany invades Czechoslovakia

26 MAY Withdrawal of British troops from Dunkirk, France

10 JUNE Italy enters war, declaring war on Britain and France

1940
JANUARY FEBRUARY MARCH APRIL MAY JUNE

23 JANUARY First breakthrough on Enigma code at Station X

10 MAY Fall of France

10 MAY Winston Churchill becomes prime minister of Great Britain

14 JUNE Germany takes over Paris

1941
JANUARY FEBRUARY MARCH APRIL MAY JUNE

MARCH Armed German ship *Krebs* is captured. On board are Enigma machines and code books, allowing the German naval code to be broken.

22 JUNE Operation Barbarossa – the invasion of Russia – begins

1942
JANUARY FEBRUARY MARCH APRIL MAY JUNE

EARLY 1942 Nazis introduce a more complex cipher, but codebreakers break it by the end of the year

JUNE The Office of Strategic Services (OSS) is set up in the United States to gather intelligence in Europe

1943
JANUARY FEBRUARY MARCH APRIL MAY JUNE

APRIL–MAY Warsaw Ghetto Uprising – the largest revolt against the Nazis

1944
JANUARY FEBRUARY MARCH APRIL MAY JUNE

JANUARY Colossus, the world's first computer, is used at Bletchley Park, to help break German codes

6 JUNE D-Day landings in Normandy, France

1945
JANUARY FEBRUARY MARCH APRIL MAY JUNE

8 MAY VE Day – Victory in Europe Day

JULY	AUGUST	SEPTEMBER	OCTOBER	NOVEMBER	DECEMBER

SEPTEMBER British Government Code and Cipher School (or GC&CS) moves into Bletchley Park, also known as Station X

JULY	AUGUST	SEPTEMBER	OCTOBER	NOVEMBER	DECEMBER

1 SEPTEMBER Germany invades Poland

3 SEPTEMBER Britain declares war on Germany

JULY	AUGUST	SEPTEMBER	OCTOBER	NOVEMBER	DECEMBER

16 JULY Battle of Britain begins

SEPTEMBER Japanese Purple cipher is broken by US codebreakers

JULY	AUGUST	SEPTEMBER	OCTOBER	NOVEMBER	DECEMBER

8 DECEMBER US declares war on Japan

JULY	AUGUST	SEPTEMBER	OCTOBER	NOVEMBER	DECEMBER

JULY	AUGUST	SEPTEMBER	OCTOBER	NOVEMBER	DECEMBER

8 SEPTEMBER Italy surrenders to the Allies

13 OCTOBER Italy declares war on Germany

JULY	AUGUST	SEPTEMBER	OCTOBER	NOVEMBER	DECEMBER

25 AUGUST Paris is freed

JULY	AUGUST	SEPTEMBER	OCTOBER	NOVEMBER	DECEMBER

6 AUGUST Atomic bomb dropped on Hiroshima, Japan

9 AUGUST Atomic bomb dropped on Nagasaki, Japan

15 AUGUST VJ Day – Victory over Japan Day

Glossary

agent person who works, often in secret, to obtain information for a government

Allies countries, such as Britain, France, the Soviet Union and the United States, that fought against the Axis Powers

atomic bomb bomb that produces an extremely powerful explosion when atoms are split apart

Axis Powers countries, including Germany, Italy and Japan, which were the enemies of the Allies

character letter or symbol

cipher system of using letters to stand for other letters to create seemingly random messages. The messages can only be read if someone knows how the cipher was created and what the letters or symbols mean.

code system of replacing particular words or numbers with others so as to disguise the original message

cryptanalyst person who decodes messages

cryptography writing or solving codes

decipher change a coded message into its original text

front in war, the region where opposing armed forces are fighting each other in battle

handler person who directs what a spy does

intelligence secret information that has political or military value, including that gained by working out what coded messages mean

invade forcibly enter a country or area with the aim of controlling it

Morse code system of dots and dashes that stand for letters of the alphabet

Nazi member of the National Socialist German Workers' Party. The party was led by Adolf Hitler.

network group of people linked by a common aim

occupied country country that is under the control of another. In World War II, Nazi Germany occupied other countries, including Poland.

propaganda information, usually of a biased or misleading nature, used to persuade people to believe in a particular political cause or point of view

recruit persuade someone to join a particular group or organization

scramble mix up

secure in communication, safely and in secret

Soviet Union Union of Soviet Socialist Republics (USSR), the communist country that existed from 1922 until 1991. Present-day Russia was part of the Soviet Union.

spy another name for an agent

surrender give in to a stronger person or force

sympathizer someone who supports a political organization or set of ideas

teleprinter typewriter that sends and receives messages, through the telephone system or by other means

Find out more

BOOKS

Codes and Codebreaking (Spies and Spying), Andrew Langley (Franklin Watts, 2009)

Secret War, Ann Kramer (Franklin Watts, 2011)

Spies (Horrible Histories), Terry Deary (Scholastic, 2013)

Spying, Henry Brook (Usborne, 2013)

The Second World War, Henry Brook (Usborne, 2013)

World War II (Tony Robinson's Weird World of Wonders), Tony Robinson (Macmillan, 2013)

WEBSITE

www.bbc.co.uk/schools/primaryhistory/world_war2
Learn more about World War II on this BBC website.

PLACES TO VISIT

The Mansion
Bletchley Park
Sherwood Drive
Bletchley
Milton Keynes, MK3 6EB
www.bletchleypark.org.uk

Bletchley Park is the place where so many codes were created and broken in World War II. It was highly secret during the war but is now open to the public.

The Imperial War Museum (**www.iwm.org.uk**) has several buildings around the country, including:
Churchill War Rooms
Clive Steps
King Charles Street
London, SW1A 2AQ

IWM London
Lambeth Road
London, SE1 6HZ

IWM North
The Quays
Trafford Wharf Road
Manchester, M17 1TZ

FURTHER RESEARCH

- See if you can find out more about some of the other spies who worked during World War II.
- Explore the relationship between the "grand alliance" of Britain, the United States and the Soviet Union.
- You could also try to learn more about World War II in general. You could investigate what happened at home during the war, for example what it was like to live with rationing. See if you can find out who Doctor Carrot was!

Index